THE
WORKPLACE
BURNOUT WORKBOOK

Anxious Lotus Publications
Lake Worth, Fl 33467
Email: theanxiouslotus@gmail.com

ISBN: 978-1-7372503-4-0 (paperback)

Ordering Information:
Special discounts are available on quantity purchases by corporations, associations, and others. For details, contact info@beccapowers.com, beccapowers.com

THE WORKPLACE
BURNOUT WORKBOOK

LEARN HOW TO UNDERSTAND, IDENTIFY, AND BREAKUP WITH BURNOUT

BECCA POWERS

CONTENTS

1.

INTRODUCTION

Preventing burnout might feel impossible as you bury your head in your hands and scream silently.

Everything feels overwhelming. Your job is eating up your time and energy, you're not the parent or partner you wish you could be, the news is infuriating, and your health and wellbeing is an afterthought.

Even your mental health breaks aren't cutting it anymore. Nothing is cutting it.

You are not alone. A recent survey of 8,000 working professionals by my consulting company, Powers Peak Potential, showed that 69% of participants are actively experiencing signs and symptoms of burnout, 29% are on the verge of burnout, and only 2% of working professionals believe they are experiencing workplace health. Similarly, Deloitte published a study showing that 77% of working Americans are experiencing signs of burnout.

We are facing a burnout epidemic. But despite the widespread problem, there are few solutions to treating or preventing burnout. We are focused on trudging through one day to the next, instead of making each day count.

In this workbook, you will get introduced to The 5 Stages of Burnout, which will help you gain a deeper insight and understanding into burnout. These five steps will assist you with overcoming and preventing burnout. The intention of this workbook is to get this revolutionary framework in your hands now.

As I write my second book, *Breakup with Burnout,* I am quite aware that the release of the book won't be until sometime in mid to late 2023. That's just too long to wait when the information will be able to help you now. Burnout sucks. I don't want to see anyone suffer any longer than they must.

My promise to you is this workbook is tiny but mighty. The framework with this workbook is going to help you grasp the fundamentals to understanding and overcoming workplace burnout, and the survey data is going to reinforce and prove that you are not the only one suffering from signs and symptoms of burnout. Lastly, there is a self-assessment for you to take to help you gauge the level of burnout you are currently in. This will give you the blueprint you need to understand and overcome workplace burnout.

You are much more powerful than you realize. You have the inner resourcefulness to take charge and live a life you love.

2.
BECCA'S BURNOUT STORY

There I was crying on the bathroom floor at 10PM on Wednesday.

As I sat there crying, I was finally admitting to myself that things were for lack of a better word–fucked. I was depressed, depleted, and desperate for help. Before I fell hopelessly to the bathroom floor, I had been reflecting on what I jerk I had been to my kids just a few hours early.

As I took my makeup off, the scene just kept repeating in my head. I recalled walking through the front door, purse on my right shoulder, running on empty after several back-to-back 12-hour bad days at work. As I walked in, my kids ran up to me bright eyed and big smiles excited to tell me about their day. Instead of greeting them with love, acceptance, and excitement, I snapped at them. I scolded them and said, "Can I put my freaking purse down first? Mommy just needs five minutes." I remember seeing how my reaction immediately hurt them. Time stopped for a minute, and it was as if I left my body and was able to have clarity from a higher perspective. Not only was I able to see their pain, but I could also feel it—and it crushed me.

I was wondering how many times I had reacted like that. I honestly had to clue and as a mother, that frightened me. How long was I there but not really there for them? I had to muster up every ounce of energy I could find to shift my attitude so I could be present. Truth be told, it was hard. I was tapped out from powering through each day as if by some miracle things were going to get better.

That night—the bathroom floor night—I fell to the bathroom floor. There I sat in my despair, feeling the most powerless I ever have in my life. At that moment, I called out to The Universe—God—insert your word of choice. I admitted that I no longer had the answers, that my solutions sucked, and that I couldn't see another way. I asked The Universe for help. It was then that I got my instant miracle. A memory came straight to my forefront of a phrase that a former VP of Sales told me, "Becca, you are the CEO of your life." It was at that moment that empowerment melted over me and I believed that within me lied the power for me to take charge of my life. I felt like a phoenix rising. I rose from the bathroom a different woman than the one that went down. That is the premise for my debut best-selling book, *Harness Your Inner CEO: Rise into Passion, Prosperity, and Empowerment.* It's my story of my rise out of burnout to help others rise out of burnout too.

By the time I was ready to make change and take charge of my life, my life was a hot mess. I was in what I now refer to as Stage 5 Burnout. I had already been diagnosed with autoimmune disease, two anxiety disorders, chronic stress, and adrenal fatigue. My most important relationships were disconnected, my marriage was on the verge of divorce, I was swimming in $40,000 dollars' worth of debt, and I had gained about 30 pounds. I knew I had a monumental mountain of task ahead of me to take me from surviving to thriving again.

Once I came to terms with my situation, my healing journey began which is detailed in Harness Your Inner CEO. I will share that I have my autoimmune disease in remission and currently testing negative. I have prioritized my well-being and as result the other areas of my life are thriving beyond what I ever thought was possible. From personal relationships to career to purpose to finances to mental and emotional health, it all improved.

Once I rose up from the bathroom floor, I made a promise to myself to never allow myself to get to that point ever again. In fulfilling that promise I had to do two things: heal from burnout and prevent it from happening again.

I knew the second thought, preventing burnout from happening again would be a bit more complex because it meant that I had to intimately understand how burnout originates, why it happens, who does it happen to, what environments trigger it, and so much more. This meant I needed to immerse myself into the shadowy center of the human psyche and I did exactly that.

I became a certified Kundalini Level 2 teacher. In that training your take a deep dive into emotional, mental, physical, and spiritual aspects of the human being. The whole process of becoming a Level 2 Teacher is multi-year and several hundred hours. In addition, I became certified as a life coach specialized in shadow beliefs and certified in trauma awareness. All of this additional education, my own real life burnout story, and my 20-year career in Fortune 500 sales and sales leadership gave me a unique perspective to form my own framework, The 5 Stages of Burnout, and then test it to see if it really helped people understand and identify burnout. After surveying 8,000 working professionals across multiple industries, I can say with confidence—and backed by data—that this model works for understanding and identifying burnout.

The Five to Thrive system is equally proven in the countless lives that have been positively transformed by implementation of the steps outlined here in this workbook. My commitment to myself to never burnout again became much bigger than me. I am very passionate about helping people understand, overcome, and prevent workplace burnout because no one deserves to feel that depleted without answers and a path to heal. This is exactly why I'm releasing this short workbook prior to the launch of the book itself. It is my hope that the information you are about to read makes a difference in your life and the lives of those that matter most to you—and helps you break up with burnout for good!

3.

HOW THIS WORKBOOK WORKS

As I mentioned above, the workbook essentially has five core parts:

THE 5 STAGES OF BURNOUT

THE WORKPLACE BURNOUT SURVEY DATA

> ### THE 5 STAGES OF BURNOUT VS. MASLOW'S HIERARCHY OF NEEDS

> ### THE FIVE STEPS TO THRIVE

> ### THE BURNOUT SELF-ASSESSMENT

Each part is designed to give you insight to that specific topic and how you can apply what you are learning to your own life. At the end of each section, I will provide a brief moment of reflection so you can—in real time—capture your thoughts and begin the breakup process. After all, that is the whole point!

INTRODUCTION TO THE BREAKUP WITH BURNOUT METHOD

Since coming up with The Breakup with Burnout Method, I have brought organizations and individuals through the same framework you will be going through. The results have been mind-blowing, truly. Organizations have been able to do a better job of recognizing and valuing their employees which has resulted in more innovation, better internal collaboration, improved WorkLife satisfaction, increased productivity, boosted revenue, and decreased attrition. Individuals have been able to reprioritize themselves to the top of the list of important things that tend to result in pay increases, promotions, job and career changes, more overall fulfillment, and are reconnected to joy and passion.

There are three core pillars in *The Breakup with Burnout Method*:

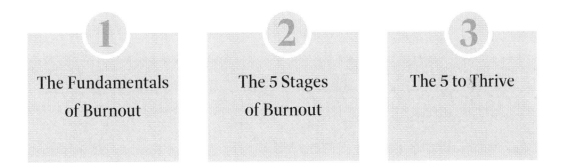

THE FUNDAMENTALS OF BURNOUT

Burnout is like a bad relationship. We can end an abusive relationship or leave a toxic job and feel temporarily empowered. When we think we have healed, we get into the next relationship or job and quickly realize after a few months—to quote Brittney Spears here– "oops, I didn't again." We find ourselves in the same pattern or cycle that we were so desperately trying to avoid. Patterns live within us and will repeat themselves until we breakup with them and change the narrative.

To be able to Breakup with Burnout for it's important to understand what the root cause of burnout is. Burnout happens because of feeling unseen, unheard, and like you don't matter for a prolonged period of time. This prolonged period starts in our childhood and forms a pattern that subconsciously repeats itself. This repeated pattern is a program inside us that seeks its execution through our environments. This burnout program's mission is to keep us safe and secure by mirroring what survival protocols worked best to get our needs for love and approval met in our childhood. The irony here is, the default program that allowed us to thrive best as a kid is the very same program that is sending some folks to their grave.

To get the most value out of this workbook, my recommendation is to play full out. With it being intentionally short, the goal is for you to participate in each part so that you can start breaking up with burnout and feeling better today!

LET'S REFLECT

To get to the root cause of burnout, let's identify when you have felt unseen, unheard, and like you don't matter while at work.

Unseen

When was that last time you felt unseen at work, what happened?

_____

_____

_____

What were the circumstances?

_____

_____

_____

Who was involved?

_____

_____

_____

_____

And, why did it make you feel unseen?

_____

_____

_____

Unheard

When was that last time you felt unheard at work, what happened?

_____

_____

_____

_____

_____

What were the circumstances?

_____

_____

_____

Who was involved?

_____

_____

_____

_____

And, why did it make you feel unseen?

_____

_____

_____

_____

Don't Matter

When was that last time you felt like you don't matter at work, what happened?

_____

_____

_____

_____

What were the circumstances?

_____

_____

_____

_____

Who was involved?

_____

_____

_____

_____

And, why did it make you feel like you don't matter?

_____

_____

_____

Early Childhood

What memory from your childhood stands out the most when you think of feeling unseen, unheard or like you don't matter, what happened?

_____

_____

_____

_____

What were the circumstances?

_____

_____

_____

_____

Who was involved?

_____

_____

_____

_____

And, why did it make you feel unseen, unheard, or like you don't matter?

_____

_____

_____

_____

The Pattern

Now that you have written a few scenarios down that could be attributing to your burnout, let's see if you can identify a pattern.

What are some commonalities within the scenarios you wrote down?

_____

_____

_____

_____

Congratulations!

You did some of the hardest work we are going to do in this workbook – which is identifying what burnout looks like for you. While the signs and symptoms for burnout are typically similar for most folks, the root cause that ignites burnout is unique to the individual. Understanding your burnout story is the first step to creating lasting change.

Awareness is the key to change – without awareness we can't break patterns. With awareness we can create meaningful and lasting change. This work you did was super important to the road ahead, great job!

THE 5 STAGES OF BURNOUT

What makes this model unique is that it helps you see and understand how burnout starts and where it takes root.

As you begin to get more intimate insights on burnout, you will find that Stage 1 and Stage 2 typically go unnoticed or are easily dismissed by us and others. What the survey revealed is that most people acknowledge they are burnt out when they are in Stage 3 or higher. However, the data shows that 88% of working professionals are experiencing Stage 1 of Burnout, The Unders, and 89% of working professionals are experiencing Stage 2 of Burnout, The Overs. This data is alarming because it means that 98% of working professionals are being impacted by burnout on some level. My goal is to get this model in front of as many people as possible so that we can begin to acknowledge burnout early and prevent the signs and symptoms of burnout from destroying people's lives. Instead, we now have language around burnout allowing you to advocate for your own well-being and create a WorkLife you love.

With that said, it's now that time. Let's dive into the **5 Stages of Burnout!**

STAGE 1: THE UNDERS

Burnout starts in The Unders. Out of the 8,000 working professionals surveyed, 88% are experiencing two or more of The Unders for an extended period. When The Unders are triggered—especially more than one—it activates our biggest fears of feeling unseen, unheard, and as if we don't matter.

THE 5 PRIMARY UNDERS ARE:

Undervalued, Underrecognized, Underappreciated, Underpaid, and Underestimated

LET'S REFLECT

List up to 3 Unders that you are currently experiencing at work.

_____

_____

_____

What's happening at work that's making you feel The Unders?

_____

_____

_____

_____

_____

STAGE 2: THE OVERS

Once The Unders and our subconscious fears are triggered, it then activates our need to protect ourselves. Our shadow beliefs such as "not being good enough," "not being worthy," "not being loveable," "I am not safe" and "there's something wrong with me" are a few examples of what gets triggered from The Unders. When these are triggered, we try to overcompensate to prove or show someone that we are not these things in order to keep ourselves safe from emotional or physical harm. In burnout it shows up as The Overs.

THE 5 PRIMARY OVERS ARE:

Overstressed, Overthinking, Overworked,
Overcommitted, and Overwhelmed

LET'S REFLECT

List up to 3 Overs that you are currently experiencing at work.

_____

_____

_____

_____

What impact are The Overs having on the way you feel?

_____

_____

_____

_____

STAGE 3: QUESTIONING BELONGING

Once The Unders and The Overs are presenting themselves in a varied combination for an extended time—especially in the workplace—all the extra effort overcompensating and going unacknowledged causes the individual to question their belonging to the organization. This is where the individual becomes less engaged at work and in meetings. They begin to power through their workdays rather than feeling like they are a part of the greater whole and feel unwanted and/or out of place.

LET'S REFLECT

When you think of staying with your organization, what comes up for you?

_____

_____

_____

_____

When you think of leaving your organization, what comes up for you?

_____

_____

_____

_____

STAGE 4: DISHARMONY IN THE BODIES

When burnout stages 1 thru 3 are lived for months or longer, we begin to see it cause disruption and disharmony in our lives. When powering through begins to cause pain, you are 100% in the signs and symptoms of burnout. The health of one if not more of the 5 Bodies will be impacted. There are five primary areas that are needed for people to thrive and be happy at work and in life. When Stage 4 is activated these areas of our life have received an invitation for disruption.

THE 5 PRIMARY BODIES ARE:

Emotional, Mental, Physical, Spiritual, and Financial

LET'S REFLECT

List up to 3 of the 5 Primary Bodies that feel the most compromised right now.

_____

_____

_____

_____

_____

What stands out as the biggest problem or disharmony right now and why?

_____

_____

_____

_____

_____

STAGE 5: DEVASTATION OF THE D'S

After living in burnout stages 1 thru 4 for months or even years, the Devastation of the D's are inevitable. These include depression, disconnected relationships with friends and family, divorce, debt, drugs (prescription and recreational), drinking, disease, and on the severe side…death.

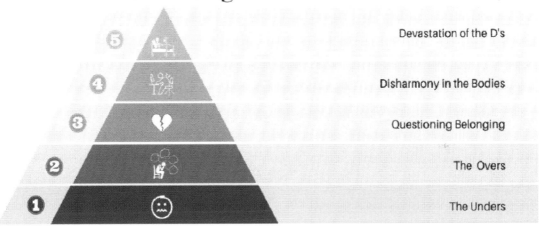

LET'S REFLECT

List up to 3 D's that are resonating as a current truth for you or that are on the horizon if something doesn't change.

_____

_____

_____

_____

_____

What stands out as the biggest problem or disharmony right now and why?

_____

_____

_____

_____

_____

LET'S REFLECT

Now that you have read through The 5 Stages of Burnout, take a quick moment to write down your current thoughts.

What is standing out for you the most after reading through The 5 Stages of Burnout? How can understanding The 5 Stages of Burnout help you in the current situation?

_____

_____

_____

_____

_____

_____

5

THE WORKPLACE BURNOUT SURVEY RESULTS

KEY FINDINGS #1

The Unders and Overs are the Starting Point of Burnout

Survey shows that on average 88% of the surveyors were experiencing one or more of The Unders.

An interesting statistic from the survey, 89% of non-leaders surveyed were experiencing one or more of The Overs. Surveyors that reported to be in leadership positions experienced a higher level of The Overs at an astonishing 94%.

After analyzing the data to find out why The Overs were reported higher than The Unders, the answer became clear. A person can experience as a minimum of one Under and produce up to five Overs. Although that example is the extreme we did commonly find four Overs for every two Unders.

Thus, reinforcing that the root cause of burnout truly is our biggest fears and deepest wounds being triggered.

KEY FINDINGS #2

The Workplace was the #1 Source of Burnout

Surveyors reported out of the options of workplace, home, or both of being the source of the burnout, The workplace received the highest ranking by a landslide coming in at 64%, followed by both 31% and home being 5%.

Some other interesting statistics are that of the surveyors only 38% were working parents. A number that I thought would be much higher.

Lastly, 72% of surveyors identified themselves as her, 20% him, and 8% them.

The data shows that burnout is officially everyone's problem—including the employers. Healing and recovering from burnout is everyone's responsibility.

On page 51, I will share tips to overcome burnout and help transition you from surviving to thriving again.

KEY FINDINGS #3
98% are Either in or on the Verge of Burnout

When I first read the results, I had to double check the data to ensure it was correct. When I realized that the data was correct, I began to cry.

The reason for the tears is that 98% of working professionals are either in or on the verge of burnout. This means that 98% of people are suffering in some form or another.

This correlates with other reports by the CDC and other agencies, that has been done on the rise of depression, heart disease, cancer, autoimmune disease, addiction, and death including suicide as reported.

Specifically, the survey results show that 69% of participants are actively in burnout and 29% have burnout on the horizon. This data aligns to a recent survey by Deloitte that showed 77% of working professionals are experiencing signs and symptoms of burnout. Whether it's 69% or 77% the numbers are staggering—and revealing that burnout is real.

6.

VISUAL SURVEY WORKPLACE DATA

BREAKUP WITH BURNOUT

RESULTS OF THE WORKPLACE
BURNOUT SURVEY

 SIGNS OF
WORKPLACE
BURNOUT

 SIGNS OF
WORKPLACE
HEALTH

PRIMARY JOB TYPES

	UNDERS AVG.*	OVERS AVG.*
LEADERSHIP	88%	94%
INDEPENDENT CONTRIBUTOR	88%	89%
OTHER	90%	91%

*UNDERS: UNDERESTIMATED, UNDERVALUED, UNDERPAID, UNDERAPPRECIATED, UNDERRECOGNIZED

*OVERS: UOVERTHINKING, OVERWORKED, OVERSTRESSED, OVERWHELMED, OVERCOMMITED

BURNOUT PERCENTAGES

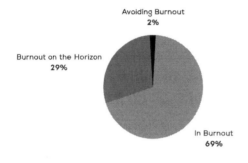

Avoiding Burnout
2%

Burnout on the Horizon
29%

In Burnout
69%

> TOTAL PERCENTAGE OF WORKING PROFESSIONALS EXPERIENCING SYMPTOMS OF BURNOUT

OTHER BURNOUT STATISTICS

WORKING PARENTING

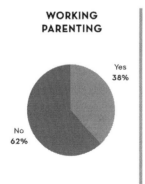

Yes
38%

No
62%

SEXUAL IDENTIFICATION

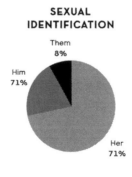

Them
8%

Him
71%

Her
71%

SOURCE OF BURNOUT

Both
31%

Home
5%

Wor
649

LET'S REFLECT

Now that you have read through The Workplace Burnout Survey results, take a quick moment to write down your current thoughts.

What is standing out for you the most after reading survey results? How can you use this data to help you today?

_____

_____

_____

_____

_____

_____

7.

THE 5 STAGES OF BURNOUT VS. MASLOW'S HIERARCHY OF NEEDS

I have a saying that data drives decisions.

Data also empowers an individual to take calculated action in the direction of a successful outcome. During the research process, another very important connection was observed. The 5 Stages of Burnout are the shadow opposite Maslow's Hierarchy of Needs. Why is this observation important? Maslow's Hierarchy of Needs is a proven model accepted in psychology and is even used by motivational giant, Tony Robbins, to illustrate what is required for a human being to thrive. Maslow's model provides the sequential order of how our needs should be met for us to live more healthy, happy, and fulfilled lives.

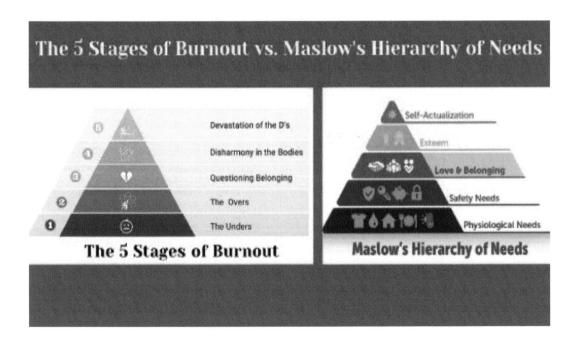

To use an example to further explain the importance of this: when Maslow's Need 1, physiological needs are rattled or not being met it triggers Stage 1 of Burnout, The Unders. To take this a step further, let's say the Sally has been with her company for 6 months as has been loving it. Then, from what feels like out-of-the-blue for Sally, her peer, Joe, suddenly gets a promotion. This rattles Sally's homeostasis, and she begins to feel insecure in her role. This insecurity makes Sally feel as though her basic needs being met are at jeopardy since she was not promoted. With her insecurity being triggered Sally feels unseen, unheard, and like she doesn't matter.

As a result, Sally begins to feel undervalued, underrecognized, and underappreciated. Stage 1 of The 5 Stages of Burnout has been activated by Need 1 of Maslow's Hierarchy of Needs being at jeopardy of not being met. From there, the stages and needs stay parallel. When a need is jeopardized that corresponding stage of burnout is activated. As we move into the next phase of overcoming burnout this knowledge will be extremely helpful as we will use Maslow's Hierarchy of Needs as a guidepost to heal burnout. We will start by addressing Need 1/Stage 1. Then, we will progress sequentially through all five needs/stages.

Now that we have a foundation for The 5 Stages of Burnout vs. Maslow's Hierarchy of

Needs, let's take a deep look at it in a side-by-side comparison.

BURNOUT STAGE	MASLOW'S NEED
Burnout Stage 1: The Unders (basic security is rattled)	Maslow's Need 1: Physiological
Burnout Stage 2: The Overs (safety is questioned)	Maslow's Need 2: Safety
Burnout Stage 3: Questioning Belonging	Maslow's Need 3: Belonging
Burnout Stage 4: Disharmony in the Bodies	Maslow's Need 4: Esteem
Burnout Stage 5: Death/Disease/ Depression	Maslow's Need 5: Self-Actualization

LET'S REFLECT

Now that you have a better understanding of The 5 Stages of Burnout, Maslow's Hierarchy of Needs, and how they correlate to each other, take a quick moment to write down your current thoughts.

What is standing out for you the most after reading the correlation between The 5 Stages of Burnout and Maslow's Hierarchy of Needs? How can understanding the correlation help you in the current situation?

_____

_____

_____

_____

_____

_____

_____

_____

_____

_____

_____

_____

_____

8.
THE FIVE TO THRIVE

In the last section, we talked about starting the process to breakup with burnout and in doing so we would begin by focusing on getting our needs met.

When we start exploring the healing path out of burnout, we will be focusing on what you can do for yourself rather than what others can do for you. Afterall, you are the only one that can truly meet your own needs. Your needs will get met by the choices that you make. The key is that we want to make more conscious choices so that our choices empower us rather than disempower us.

The Power of Choice

Choice has two paths. Our choices either empower us or disempower us, they support us or sabotage us, they help us or they hurt us. I'm sure you get the picture! This is so important because according to Psychology Today, we make 35,000 choices a day that's insane. Depending on the resources an astonishing 90% to 95% of our choices are subconscious—meaning we are making them without thinking of them. Let's imagine that these auto-pilot subconscious choices are coming from a burnout state of mind—ouch! So many decisions are disempowering, sabotaging, and hurting us because we aren't consciously making them, or we are making them in fear because our feeling of security and safety has been jeopardized. The goal is to make more conscious choices where you are checking in with yourself (ex: "Does the decision help or hurt me?"). Just like an ex-lover that we keep going back to, our jobs and careers can be very similar. We end up settling and staying because change is scary, or we quit and then end up at a job that sucks the life out of us again. With The Power of Choice in your toolkit, it will help empower you to make more choices that help and serve you. You will need that faith in yourself and your ability to make healthy decisions to breakup with burnout for good—just like that ex-lover!

Now that we have The Power of Choice in our toolkit, let's get to this breakup!

LET'S REFLECT

Can you remember a recent decision or choice you made that may have disempowered you or sabotaged you in some way? If so, what was it and how did it not support you?

_____

_____

_____

_____

Can you remember a recent decision or choice you made that may have empowered you or served you in some way? If so, what was it and how did it support you?

_____

_____

_____

_____

STEP 1: PERMISSION TO PRIORITIZE YOURSELF

As we look at Maslow's first need of physiological needs like food, water, being able to breathe, a roof over your head, you can see in modern times this boils down to: are you secure at your job? In effort to ensure our foundational needs are met we want to establish our value. Often—especially if you find yourself juggling exhausting days between work and family—prioritizing your needs does not even make the top five list of things you need to tend to. This is the pattern we need to breakup, prioritizing the needs of others before we prioritize ourselves.

What I have found is that service-based and high achieving folks like leaders, salespeople, first responders, healthcare professionals, teachers, entrepreneurs, influencers, as a few examples, seem to put the desire to make a positive impact or to make a difference before themselves.

While the intention is noble and for good cause, it's this very act of not prioritizing your needs that leaves you susceptible to Stage 1 Burnout. This effort over time puts you in a survival state rather than a thriving state.

Giving yourself permission to prioritize yourself first is non-negotiable. Getting your basic needs met is a must just as we see in Maslow's Hierarchy of Needs, which means you are entitled to breathe easy without massive levels of stress—because this is your human right. When you begin to consider your needs just as much as you consider the needs of the business and your family and then act on prioritizing them, your energy will shift from a survival state to a thriving state. To get there, you must give yourself permission for it to be safe and OK for you to be #1 on your list of important things.

BREAKUP WITH BURNOUT LIFE HACK #1:

Stop prioritizing others before yourself and start prioritizing yourself.

LET'S REFLECT

If you get honest with yourself, does putting yourself at the top of the priority list feel uncomfortable? If so, why?

_____

_____

_____

_____

_____

_____

_____

STEP 2: BECOME A BOUNDARY NINJA

Looking at Maslow's Need 2 being safe, it makes sense that we accidently abandon ourselves in trying to get that need met. One way we do that is tending to the needs of the business and/or the family before we tend to our own needs. Because when we feel validated and approved of it makes us feel safe. This is an outdated program. We need the validation and approval from our parents to survive and be safe. It's a learned behavior. The thing is we are no longer seven years old, and we need to breakup with the pattern. It no longer supports our highest health and potential.

The hardest thing to do when you are so accustomed to saying YES is learning to say NO. When you are in burnout there has been a pattern established. The pattern is not honoring your own time, space, and well-being as a priority. You often find yourself overextended, overwhelmed, and overstressed and wish someone would rescue you and relieve you of some of your responsibilities. You want someone to see you, acknowledge how much you are doing, and recognize just how exhausted you are. This person you are longing for is YOU.

Practicing saying no to others when you are so used to saying yes is hard. Change is scary and yet on the other side of it is our best life. Setting boundaries will take practice so have patience with yourself. Once you get the hang of it, you will learn that saying yes to your health, happiness, and well-being requires you to say no to other people and commitments. This boundary of saying no or not right now to someone so that you can say yes to yourself is the biggest baddest boundary you can set in your life. This will keep you from overcompensating and keep your energy with you!

BREAKUP WITH BURNOUT LIFE HACK #2:

Stop saying yes to everyone and everything and start saying yes to yourself first—then you can say yes to the others if it feels good for you. This is the biggest baddest boundary you could ever set.

LET'S REFLECT

If you get honest with yourself, how often do you say yes to things that you know will overextend yourself? How does this ultimately make you feel?

_____

_____

_____

_____

If it were true that everything in your life thrives when you thrive, how would saying no instead of yes give you more time, space, and energy?

_____

_____

_____

_____

STEP 3: COLLABORATION CREATES CONNECTION

As we look back on Maslow's Need 3: Belonging, it makes sense why we get some sickness when we enter Stage 3 of Burnout: Questioning Belonging. This is because it's an essential human need to belong to something, to be part of a team, or part of a tribe if you think about our primal history. Besides our families, our workplace is essentially fulfilling the need of belonging since it is the place, we spend the majority of our time. When we don't feel seen, heard and like we matter and have already been through The Unders and The Overs, our sense of belonging is in question and as you have learned throughout this workbook begins to impact our overall health and sanity.

It's essential for your healing that you have a sense of belonging and collaboration with others will help build a feeling of support and community for you. When you are unable to get this need fulfilled from work, you need to build your own team. Building a team of people from mentors to coaches to supportive friends that are invested in you will create a feeling of community. This increases your feeling of connection and helps you feel more valued, seen, and appreciated. Helping you breakup with burnout and giving you more energy to thrive.

BREAKUP WITH BURNOUT LIFE HACK #3:

> Stop searching for acceptance and validation from people at work and start building a team of people to support you and who already accept and value you for who you are.

LET'S REFLECT

If you get honest with yourself, do the people you associate with the most support you or add to your stress? Write a few ways that you either supported or not supported?

_____

_____

_____

_____

If it were true that everything in your life thrives when you thrive, who in your network could you lean on for positive support?

_____

_____

_____

_____

STEP 4: ALLOW YOUR SELF'S TO RISE

Let's look at Maslow's Need 4: Esteem. Before we do, I want to rewind a bit and bring back to the forefront that Maslow's Hierarchy of Needs is a proven framework for what needs need to be met for human beings to thrive. As we progress through the needs, you will see that once a person feels secure in their basic needs being met, they feel physically and emotionally safe, their sense of belonging and support is strong, it is then that a person can feel confident in their own skin and really begin to allow what I refer to as the Self's to rise. This is your self-esteem, your self-worth, your self-love, your self-acceptance, your sense of self, your ability to self-nourish, etc.

When we look at Stage 4 Burnout: Disharmony in the Bodies, it makes sense why we get into this start because without feeling seen, having to overcompensate to exhaustion, then not feeling a part of something greater, it is a natural next step for a human to feel worthless, hopeless, and even powerless. It is here that we begin to accept doom and gloom, change feels impossible, and we begin to tolerate the intolerable. It is in this place that disharmony takes over and our mental and emotional health is severely compromised.

As we embrace our esteem, here is the fourth step to breakup with burnout. We want to focus on our strengths, our talents, our passions, and what lights us up. As you continue to honor yourself and your well-being your confidence is going to increase making it easier and easier for you to prioritize yourself, set and keep boundaries, and your new vibe will attract more of your supportive tribe. All of these are so important to creating a WorkLife that thrives! Remember, in this step, it's about embracing your awesomeness and owning all of you—the messy and the magical.

BREAKUP WITH BURNOUT LIFE HACK #4:

> Stop dimming your own light and playing small and start harnessing your power to allow all of your Self's an opportunity to rise!

LET'S REFLECT

If you get honest with yourself, is your self-worth, self-confidence, and self-esteem impacted by your current situation? If so, how?

_____

_____

_____

_____

If it were true that everything in your life thrives when you thrive, what would be different at work if your self-worth, self-confidence, and self-esteem were high?

_____

_____

_____

_____

_____

STEP 5: EMBRACE YOUR BECOMING

As we take a last look at Maslow's Hierarchy of Needs, we see that the final need is self-actualization. This is our truest potential or full expression of love, purpose, and fulfillment. In Kundalini yoga, we call this Sat Nam, truth is your name. Meaning that you the truth of your identity is already within you, and you just need to call it forward. For a person to really rise into who they were born to become, the previous four needs need to be met otherwise it leaves a person questioning themselves and whether it's safe to be all they were meant to be. As we pull from the last step of allowing your Self's to rise this will boost your confidence and help you embrace your becoming.

Stage 5 Burnout, The Devastation of the D's, is the mirror opposite of self-actualization. We find in Stage 5 Burnout that death is in three categories is up amongst working professionals and the three categories are: heart disease, cancer, and suicide. This is why it is so important to heal one step at a time. If you are in Stage 4 and Stage 5 of Burnout, we need to get you in a space of healing and overcoming it as soon as possible. One small conscious step at a time is how you start to recover. Now that we have seen the positive outcomes from going through The 5 Steps to Breakup with Burnout, we can see why it is worth creating a new way of being. Because living a life that is rooted in you feeling good and trusting your own self-reliance is the way to go!

When more decisions come from the place of strengthened self-esteem you become the person you were born to be and begin to level up in multiple areas of life. In addition to leveling up, other areas of your life begin to thrive in the most miraculous and unexpected ways. You will find remissions in autoimmune disease and cancer, you will find financial abundance where there was once lack, you will find connection and depth in your relationships when they used to be superficial and surface level. As your life begins to regenerate, embracing your becoming is essential. You will need to harness the gifts, strengths, and talents to rise into the person you were born to be so you can make the difference you were born to make!

BREAKUP WITH BURNOUT LIFE HACK #5:

Stop second guessing yourself and start embracing all that you were born to be—especially your gifts and talents.

LET'S REFLECT

If you get honest with yourself, do you hold yourself and your potential back? If so, why?

_____

_____

_____

_____

If it were true that everything in your life thrives when you thrive, how could unleashing your potential impact your life and the life of others?

_____

_____

_____

_____

MORE REFLECTION

Now that you have read through The 5 Steps to Breakup with Burnout, take a quick moment to write down your current thoughts.

What is standing out for you the most after reading through The 5 Steps to Breakup with Burnout? What is one choice you can make today that will empower you?

_____

_____

_____

_____

_____

_____

_____

9.
THE WORKPLACE BURNOUT SELF-ASSESSMENT

Rate each one below | Never = 1 • Sometimes = 2 • Aways = 3

STAGE 1: THE UNDERS

How often do you feel The Unders?

	Never	Sometimes	Always
Undervalued	○	○	○
Underapprevciated	○	○	○
Underestimated	○	○	○
Underpaid	○	○	○
Underrecognized	○	○	○

Put a ★ next to The Under you feel the most.

Section Score: _____

STAGE 2: THE OVERS

How often do you feel The Overs?

	Never	Sometimes	Always
Overthinking	◯	◯	◯
Overstressing	◯	◯	◯
Overworking	◯	◯	◯
Overwhelming	◯	◯	◯
Overcommitting	◯	◯	◯

Put a ★ *next to The Over you feel the most.*

Section Score: _____

STAGE 3: QUESTIONING BELONGING

How often do you feel yourself Questioning Belonging at work?

	Never	Sometimes	Always
Feel Unwanted	○	○	○
Feel unseen	○	○	○
Feel unheard	○	○	○
Feel disconnected from the team	○	○	○
Feel like you don't matter	○	○	○

Put a ★ *next to the Feeling you feel the most.*

Section Score: _____

STAGE 4: DISHARMONY IN THE BODIES

How often do you feel Disharmony in the Body?

	Never	Sometimes	Always
Emotional discomfort	◯	◯	◯
Physical discomfort	◯	◯	◯
Mental discomfort	◯	◯	◯
Spiritual disconnection	◯	◯	◯
Financial discomfort	◯	◯	◯

Put a ★ *next to The Body you feel the most disharmony.*

Section Score: _____

STAGE 5: THE DEVASTATION OF THE D'S

	Never	Sometimes	Always
Deep depression	○	○	○
Disconnected relationships	○	○	○
Desire or need to medicate	○	○	○
Debt Stress	○	○	○
Disease or Illness	○	○	○

Put a ★ *next to The D that is impacting you the most.*

Section Score: _____

Total Score: _____

SELF-ASSESSMENT OUTCOMES

25 -35: All Clear – Congratulations, your score indicates you are avoiding burnout. It's not abnormal to experience some signs and symptoms sometimes. Keep up the good work!

36- 45 Score: Burnout Ignited - Your score indicates that signs and symptoms of burnout are becoming steady. Stage 1 and Stage 2 are activated and your flames of burnout of flirting with Stage 3.

46 – 60 Score: Active Fire – Your score indicates that you are in active burnout. This means that Stage 1 -3 are fanning the flames of your burnout fire and you're beginning to see the impact of Stage 4.

61 - 75 Score: Burnt – Your score indicates that you are burnt out. The flames of all the burnout stages are burning up your life. If you haven't gotten help yet I hope this workbook gives you some tools, you can use to start breaking up with burnout and begin healing.

LET'S REFLECT

Now that you have taken the self-assessment and seen your results, take a quick moment to write down your current thoughts.

What is standing out for you the most after completing the self-assessment? What items were starred in each section?

_____

_____

_____

_____

_____

_____

_____

_____

_____

_____

_____

_____

_____

What are some actions you can take that prioritize your well-being? What one action can you commit to?

_____

_____

_____

_____

10.

NEED MORE RESOURCES ON BURNOUT?

Breaking up with burnout will take time and commitment to stop the patterns from reoccurring and to start healing into a life full of health, happiness, and fulfillment.

In my experience from recovering from severe burnout and now helping others do the same, I have learned that healing is multi-path approached and requires patience. It may require a combination of modalities to completely heal. Don't get discouraged if one doesn't work, just try another. I will provide a few options to continue to work with me. Follow me on social media for tips, tools, resources, and more content.

@BECCAPOWERS1313

BREAKUP WITH BURNOUT ONLINE MINI-COURSE
REGULAR INVESTMENT: $98

Becca's Breakup with Burnout Method is revolutionizing how people understand, overcome, and prevent workplace burnout. Becca has developed a Breakup with Burnout Mini-Course that consists of two 30-minute video modules, this workbook, and additional worksheets to give you the tools you need to understand burnout more intimately.

Module 1:

The 5 Stages
of Burnout

Module 2:

The 5 Steps to Breakup
with Burnout

NOW $49

50% OFF

*Breakup with
Burnout Mini-Course*
Limited Time
Instant Savings

PURCHASE NOW!

GO ONLINE AND VISIT:

www.beccapowers.com/burnoutminicoursespecial

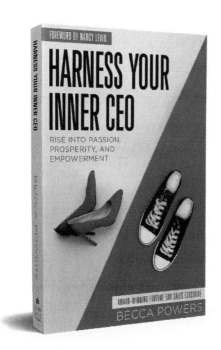

AVAILABLE AT MULTIPLE RETAILERS

You shouldn't have to choose between success and happiness!

Juggling exhausting workdays, managing kids, and giving your relationship more care than you give yourself is a recipe for misery. Instead of enjoying the fruits of your labor, you feel tired, unhealthy, and joyless.

Fortune 500 sales executive Becca Powers knows this feeling all too well. She was burned out and missing out on motherhood by prioritizing her career first. After overworking herself into autoimmune disease and anxiety disorders, her self-worth plummeted. The universe was delivering one clear message: things were fucked and needed to change.

The life of your dreams shouldn't come at an unsustainable price. *Harness Your Inner CEO* illustrates Becca›s journey from a toxic work environment, stress at home, and emotional rock bottom to living a thriving, prosperous life. With this practical yet spiritual guide for women in business, empower the confident CEO within and love life again with unstoppable prosperity and passion—without sacrificing yourself.

You'll discover:

- ⊙ The AWTaF Method, a four-step strategy to help you pause, recalibrate, reconsider, and invite possibility.

- ⊙ Your current Ladder of Self-Worth—and how to activate confidence by reorganizing its rungs and your growth mindset.

- ➡ A goal-based Vision List to find your fire, push past discomfort, and power up every day with healthier habits for productivity.

- ➡ Personal "AND" statements to bust through constricting stereotypes and embrace the strong woman you are, unapologetically.

- ➡ Tips to build a dream team that supports your new vision for your world.

As boss of your own enterprise, you can master both your magic and your messy. Get *Harness Your Inner CEO* and realign yourself to create a lifestyle that thrives!

PURCHASE NOW!

beccapowers.com/harnessyourinnerceo

Group or Private Coaching with Becca

Becca does offer group and private coaching. For more information you can call or text Team Becca at 561.463.6400 or email info@beccapowers.com

Free 7-Day Email Empowerment Challenge

Beca's 7 Day Email Empowerment Challenge will give you one action item a day to help you get unstuck and back into your groove: www.beccapowers.com/empowerment

Other Options to Help You Heal

- Traditional Therapy
- Emotional Freedom Technique (EFT)
- EMDR
- Yoga
- Kundalini Yoga
- Walking
- Running
- Private Coaching
- Group Coaching
- Meditation
- Nutrition
- Supplements

- Reading
- Acupuncture
- Lymphatic
- Massage
- New Hobbies
- Music
- Singing
- Dancing
- Painting
- Pottery
- Playing an Instrument
- Writing
- Journaling

ABOUT THE AUTHOR

Becca Powers is an award-winning Fortune 500 hi-tech sales executive, Founder and CEO of Powers Peak Potential, best-selling author, and speaker.

In her 20+ year career in sales, she's worked for large companies including Cisco, Dell, and Office Depot, achieving President's Club seven times while leading teams of 110+

and hitting $500 million in annual revenue.

Becca intimately knows the struggles that have come as a cost to her high achievements. Through nearly losing it all from extreme burnout, she was forced to discover a more supportive and sustainable path to success that she now teaches to others. She founded her consulting and coaching agency to help high achievers and high-performance teams' breakup with burnout cycles and create WorkLife success. Through workshops, seminars and her signature programs, Becca works with individuals and organizations to create sustainable change by training them to thrive from the inside out without the cost of compromise.

In addition to being a WorkLife Strategist with specialties in shadow beliefs and trauma awareness, she's also a Kundalini yoga teacher, and incorporates many holistic modalities into her programs. In 202,1 she released her best-selling book, *Harness Your Inner CEO: Rise into Passion, Prosperity, and Empowerment* to increase her ability to help others become the CEOs of their own lives.

Becca currently resides in South Florida with her husband Jermey and has 4 adult kids. For more information, visit www.beccapowers.com and tune into her podcast, The High Achievers Club on your favorite podcasting platform. Contact Team Becca at info@beccapowers.com or 561.463.6400.

Made in the USA
Columbia, SC
08 April 2023

14521526R00052